# DRUMSENSE

by

## COLIN WOOLWAY

## Volume II

### Jazz - Basic Strokes - Further Independence

The continued steps towards coordination, style and technique

Drumsense Publications
68-70 London Road, Croydon CR0 2TB
United Kingdom
www.drumsense.com

Colin Woolway uses Sonor drums, Zildjian cymbals, Vic Firth drumsticks, Aquarian drumheads, Bill Sanders practice pads and Protection Racket cases exclusively.

ISBN   978-0-9555593-0-3

DRUMSENSE Volume II 3rd edition
This Volume:
© 2007 Colin Woolway

Published by Drumsense Publications

Printed in England by Caligraving Ltd, Thetford, Norfolk

Accompanying CD:
℗ & © 2007 Colin Woolway

Recorded at: Moon Studios, Croydon, Surrey

# DRUMSENSE

## CONTENTS

### Part I - Jazz

| | |
|---|---|
| Standard Jazz Rhythm | 1 |
| Fills - Subdivision of eighth note triplets | 3 |
| Section 1 - Play around the kit | 4 |
| Section 2 - Play accents on the toms | 6 |
| Section 3 - Play accents on the cymbals | 8 |
| Jazz Independence | 10 |
| Section 1 - Right hand swing - left hand independence | 10 |
| a) Accents on the beat | 11 |
| b) Accents off the beat | 12 |
| c) Combining onbeat and offbeat accents | 13 |
| Section 2 - Right hand swing - bass drum independence | 14 |
| a) Accents on the beat | 14 |
| b) Accents off the beat | 15 |
| c) Combining onbeat and offbeat accents | 16 |
| Section 3 - Right hand swing - snare and bass drum independence | 17 |
| Section 4 - Snare and bass drum independence - variations | 18 |
| Further Independence | 19 |
| Subdivision of sixteenth notes with quarter notes on the hi hat | 19 |
| Section 1 - Play around the kit | 20 |
| Section 2 - Play accents on the toms | 22 |
| Section 3 - Play accents on the cymbals | 24 |

### PART II - Technique, Basic Strokes

| | |
|---|---|
| Technique - Basic Strokes | 26 |
| Accents and taps | 26 |
| Accents and taps, sixteenth note feel | 26 |
| Accents and taps, triplet feel | 28 |
| Accented strokes and upstrokes | 29 |
| Basic rock, accents and up strokes | 29 |
| Basic rock, sixteenth notes on the hi hat, accents and up strokes | 31 |
| Bass drum independence, accents and up strokes | 32 |
| Bass drum independence, sixteenth notes on hi hat, accents and up strokes | 33 |
| The use of upward strokes in everyday playing | 34 |
| Application of upward taps in sixteenth note fills | 34 |
| Application of upward taps in eighth note triplet fills | 37 |

# SYMBOLS USED IN THIS BOOK

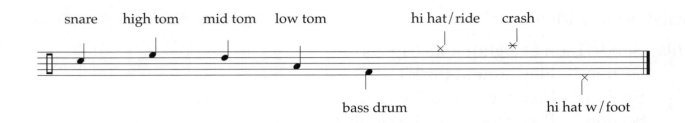

snare    high tom    mid tom    low tom         hi hat/ride    crash

bass drum                                    hi hat w/foot

## TRACK LISTINGS

Your *Drumsense* volume has an accompanying CD.

Each section in the book marked with (track 1) through to (track 22) relates to a track on the CD.

The number within the symbol tells you which track number the exercise relates to.

Each track on the CD covers one example and all its variations.

## USING THE CD

You will gain the most benefit from this book by using the CD from the very first page. This will greatly enhance your understanding of the music and enable you to hear how the patterns should sound at slow and medium tempi.

Always try to count along with the CD and listen to each example at least once before attempting it.

# Part I - Jazz

# Standard Jazz Rhythm

The first thing to learn is the standard jazz rhythm, involving ride cymbal, hi hat, bass drum and snare drum.

1. The bass drum plays four quarter notes to the bar.

2. The ride cymbal plays the jazz or *swing* rhythm.

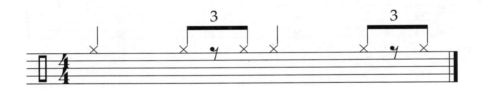

3. The snare drum plays on beats 2 and 4.

4. The hi hat, played with the left foot, is also on beats 2 and 4.

5. Now play the bass drum and ride cymbal together.

6. Now add the snare drum.

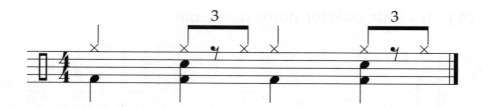

7. And finally, the hi hat. You now have the complete rhythm.

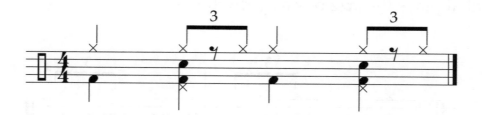

# Fills
## Subdivision of eighth note triplets

In Drumsense Volume I we looked at playing 'fills' in the two different feels: sixteenth notes - *straight feel* and eighth note triplets - *shuffle* or *swing feel*. Jazz is played in *swing feel*, so we should use eighth note triplets as a basis for playing fills.

Let's recap on the examples from **Subdivision of eighth note triplets** from Drumsense Volume I:

1.  **3   3   3   3**

2.  **6   6**

3.  **6   2   2   2**

4.  **2   2   2   6**

5.  **2   2   2   2   2   2**

## Interpretation

Section 1 - Play around the kit
Section 2 - Play accents on the toms
Section 3 - Play accents on the cymbals

# Section 1
# Play around the kit

Track 2

### 1. 3-3-3-3

So let's play a four bar phrase, using three bars of swing and one bar of fill; 3-3-3-3 around the kit.

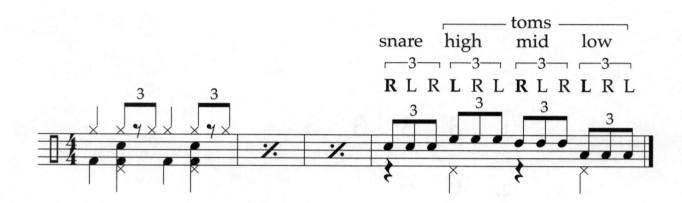

There are two main differences between the way we are playing now and the way we learnt in volume I. First, we are using the ride cymbal instead of the hi hat and second, the hi hat, played with our left foot, is keeping steady time on beats 2 and 4, even when we play the fill. We should explore the idea of keeping time with the hi hat further.

### 2. 6-6

Here is a four bar phrase with 6-6 Around the kit as a fill - notice that the left foot hi hat notes fall on the left hand notes all the time.

## 3. **6-2-2-2**

Now let's try 6-2-2-2.

## 4. **2-2-2-6**

## 5. **2-2-2-2-2-2**

Will not work around the kit unless you have five toms.

5

# Section 2
## Play accents on the toms

Always keep the hi hat, on beats 2 and 4, falling on the *left hand*.

Track ③

### 1. 3-3-3-3

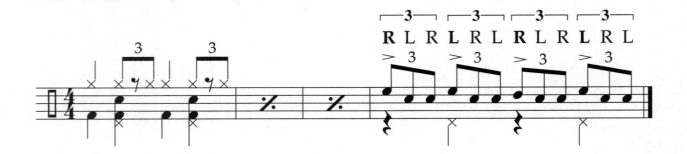

### 2. 6-6

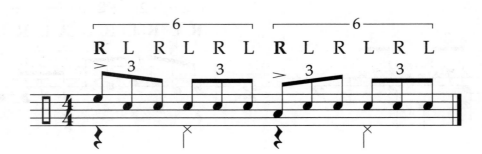

### 3. 6-2-2-2

Notice the **quarter note triplet** produced by the right hand accents, and how the hi hat falls *between* them.

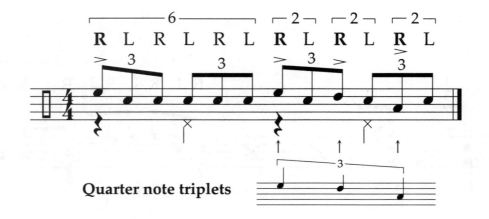

Quarter note triplets

## 4. 2-2-2-6

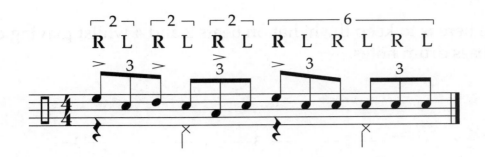

## 5. 2-2-2-2-2-2

**Quarter note triplets** across the toms, the hi hat falls *between* the accents.

# Section 3
## Play accents on crash cymbals

The challenge here is to keep the hi hat on beats 2 and 4 whilst playing cymbal crashes backed with bass drum notes.

Track 4

1. **3-3-3-3**

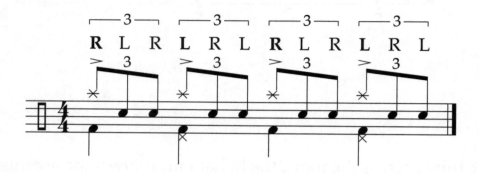

2. **6-6**

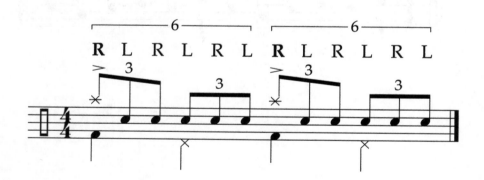

3. **6-2-2-2**

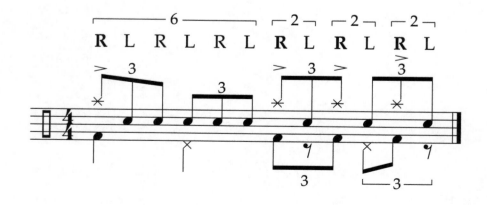

## 4. **2-2-2-6**

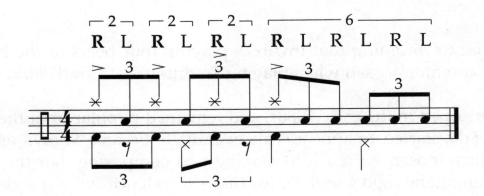

## 5. **2-2-2-2-2-2**

Once again, note how the quarter note triplets cross over the hi hat notes.

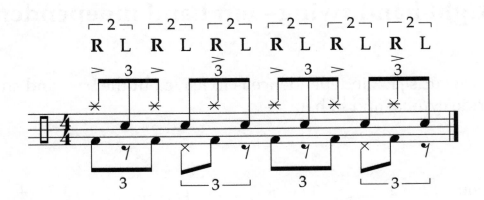

# Jazz Independence

The style of jazz drumming that involves playing four beats to the bar on the bass drum is most commonly used when playing Traditional or "Trad" jazz.

This style developed in the early 1900s, and remained popular until the 1950s, when a new form of jazz started to appear. This eventually became known as "Bebop" jazz, and had a much looser approach to playing and composing. For the drummer, this meant abandoning the rigid *four to the bar bass, snare on two and four* style.

So let's begin this section by by playing on the ride cymbal and hi hat only.

## Section 1
## Right hand swing - left hand independence

The first step towards jazz independence is to leave out the bass and snare drums, and focus on the ride cymbal and hi hat:

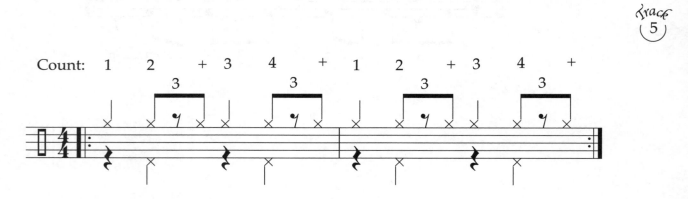

Now we are going to start playing the snare drum accents with our left hand, *against* the ride cymbal and hi hat.

# a) Accents on the beat

1. Play a left hand snare accent on the first beat of the bar, (beat 1).

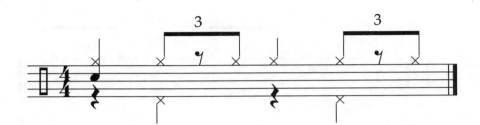

2. Play an accent on beat 2.

3. Play an accent on beat 3.

4. Play an accent on beat 4.

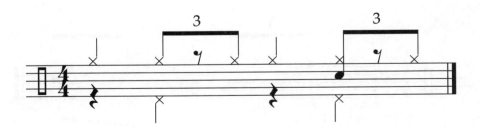

# b) Accents off the beat

1. Play a left hand snare accent *after* beat 1 (on the *'and'* of beat 1).

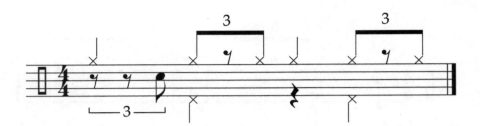

2. Play an accent *after* beat 2 (on the *'and'* of beat 2).

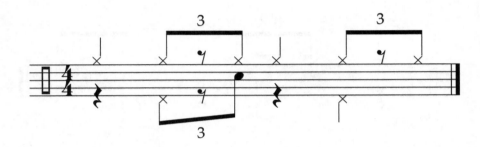

3. Play an accent *after* beat 3 (on the *'and'* of beat 3).

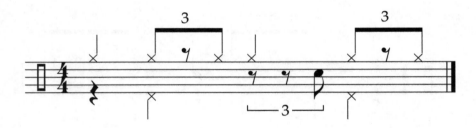

4. Play an accent *after* beat 4 (on the *'and'* of beat 4).

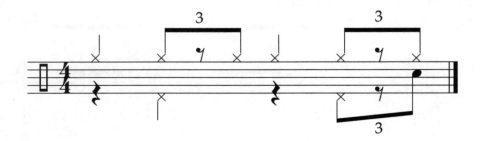

# c) Combining onbeat and offbeat accents

Now we are going to combine the two sets of accents. Each bar will have an onbeat accent, followed by an offbeat after the next quarter note.

1.  Accents on beat 1, and the *'and'* of beat 2.

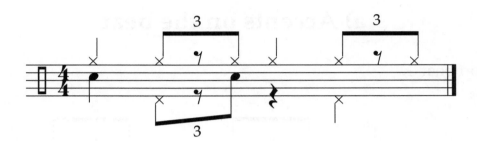

2.  Accents on beat 2, and the *'and'* of beat 3.

3.  Accents on beat 3, and the *'and'* of beat 4.

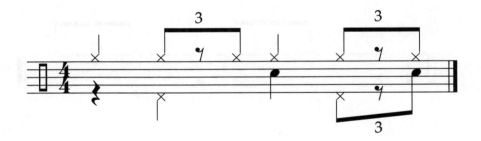

4.  Accents on beat 4, and the *'and'* of beat 1.

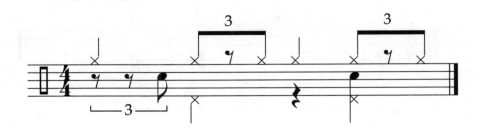

# Section 2
# Right hand swing - bass drum independence

The easiest way to develop bass drum independence in jazz is to convert all the previous snare drum exercises to bass drum exercises.

## a) Accents on the beat

Track 9

1. Bass drum on beat 1.

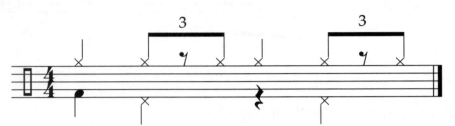

2. Bass drum on beat 2.

3. Bass drum on beat 3.

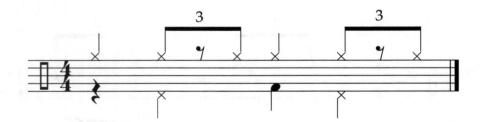

4. Bass drum on beat 4.

# b) Accents off the beat

1. Bass drum on the *'and'* of beat 1.

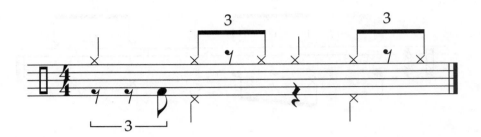

2. Bass drum on the *'and'* of beat 2.

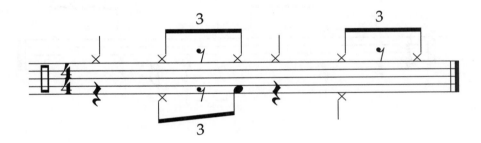

3. Bass drum on the *'and'* of beat 3.

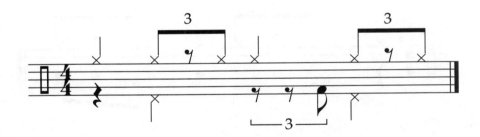

4. Bass drum on the *'and'* of beat 4.

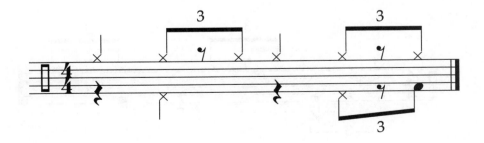

# c) Combining onbeat and offbeat accents

1. Beat 1 and the *'and'* of beat 2.

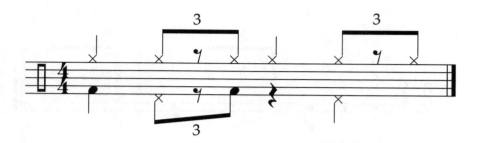

2. Beat 2 and the *'and'* of beat 3.

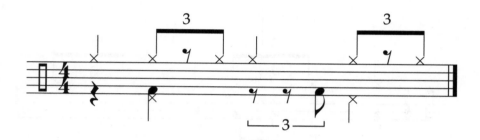

3. Beat 3 and the *'and'* of beat 4.

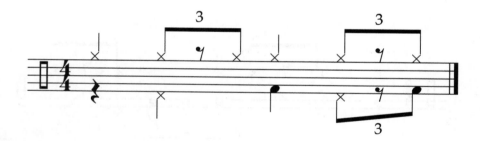

4. Beat 4 and the *'and'* of beat 1.

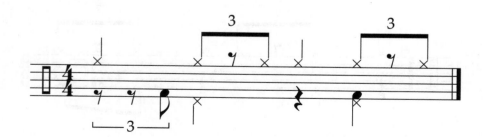

# Section 3
# Right hand swing - Snare and bass drum independence

The next step is to play musical phrases by changing 'voices', for example, alternating between snare and bass every bar. If we take the first exercise, "Beat 1 and the *'and'* of beat 2", we get this:

*Track*
(12)

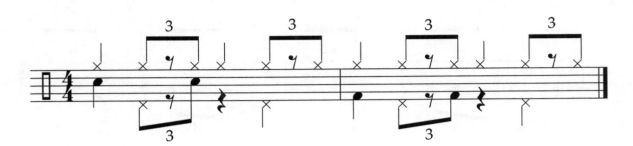

Now try: "Beat 2 and the *'and'* of beat 3".

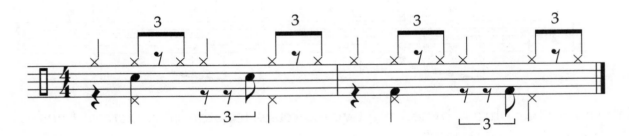

Now: "Beat 3 and the *'and'* of beat 4".

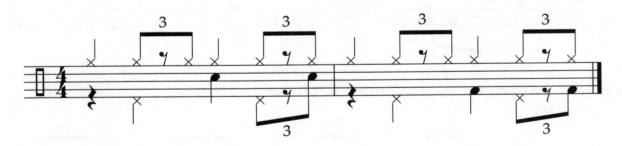

And: "Beat 4 and the *'and'* of beat 1".

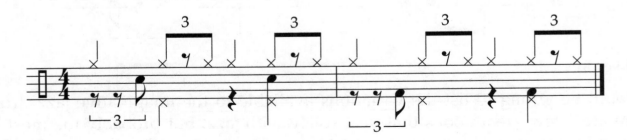

*Note: The left hand can move around the kit, playing high, mid and low toms. In this way, you can alternate "voices" rather than limbs!*

# Section 4
# Bass and snare drum independence - Variations

Here are some ideas to get you thinking and practising musically:
*The example given is always exercise 1, but do try the other exercises!*

Track (13)

1. Alternate left hand and bass every note.

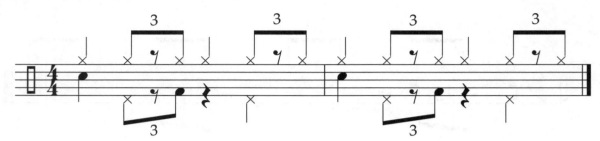

2. Alternate left hand and bass, but *invert* the exercise each time.

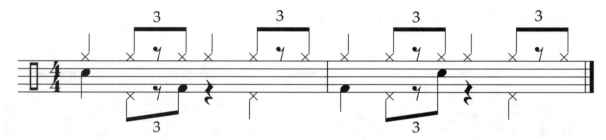

3. Make a two bar phrase by joining two exercises together. *e.g. exercise 1 and 2.*

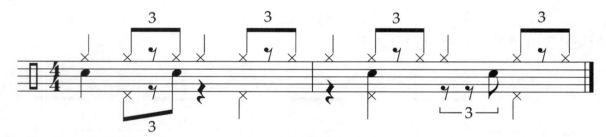

4. Play a two bar phrase, and alternate left hand and bass.

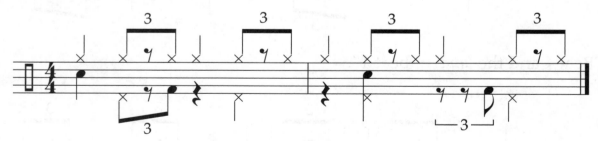

And so on.......!

It would be wrong to list the variations available to the imaginative jazz drummer. There are a few great books that deal solely with jazz, but probably the most highly praised is *Advanced Techniques for the Modern Drummer* by Jim Chapin. Similarly, it would be impossible to list all the jazz drummers of note, but a good starting point is to acknowledge the great drumming of Buddy Rich and Louis Bellson, who were both influenced by Gene Krupa.

# Further Independence
## Subdivision of sixteenth notes, with quarter notes on the hi hat

Now we should look at playing 16th note fills keeping quarter note time with the left foot on the hi hat. We will use the subdivisions from **Drumsense Volume I**, which are as follows.

## Subdivision of sixteenth notes

1. **4  4  4  4**

2. **8  8**

3. **6  2  6  2**

4. **3  3  4  6**

5. **3  3  3  3**     a) **4**

                                          b) **2  2**

                                          c) **3  1**

## Interpretation

Section 1 - Play around the kit
Section 2 - Play accents on the toms
Section 3 - Play accents on the cymbals

# Section 1
# Play around the kit

1. **4-4-4-4**

The hi hat will fall on each change of drum.

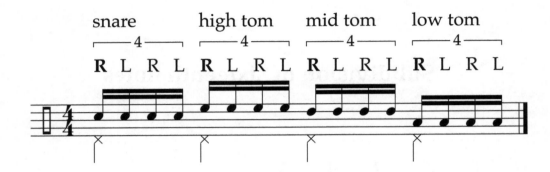

Exercise:

Try a four bar phrase, right hand playing the ride cymbal, left foot keeping quarter note time.

Example:

Try four bar phrases with all the subdivisions:

2. **8-8**

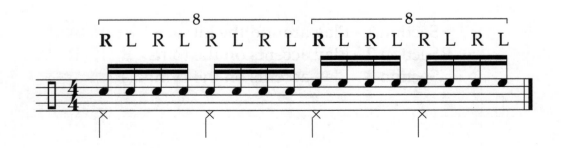

## 3. **6-2-6-2**

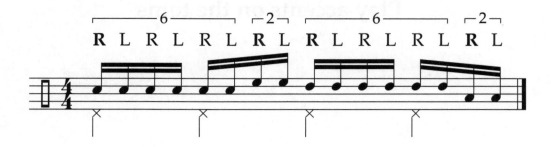

## 4. **3-3-4-6**

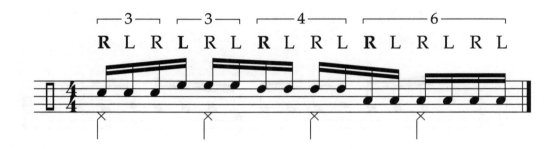

## 5a). **3-3-3-3-4**

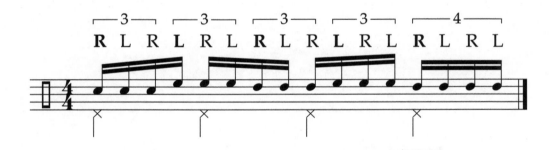

## 5b). **3-3-3-3-2-2**

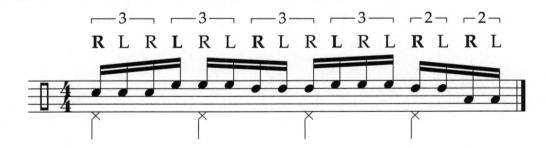

## 5c). **3-3-3-3-3-1**

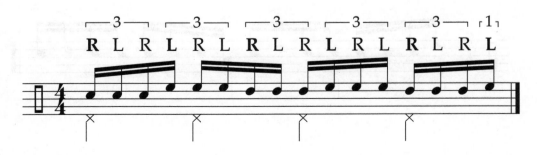

# Section 2
## Play accents on the toms

1. **4-4-4-4**

Track (15)

2. **8-8**

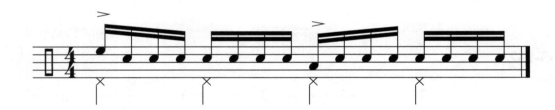

3. **6-2-6-2**

**4. 3-3-4-6**

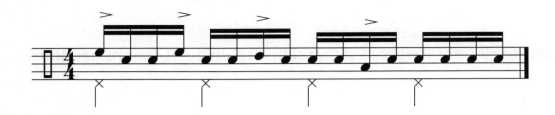

**5a) 3-3-3-3-4**

**5b) 3-3-3-3-2-2**

**5c) 3-3-3-3-3-1**

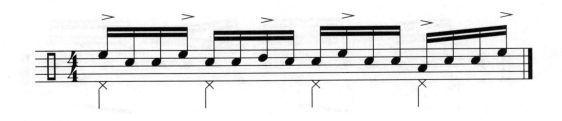

# Section 3
## Play accents on the cymbals

Take care over the right foot bass drum notes against left foot hi hat notes.

1. **4-4-4-4**

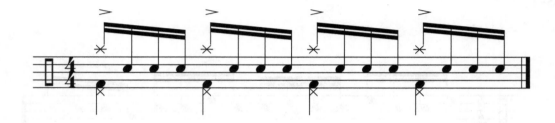

2. **8-8**

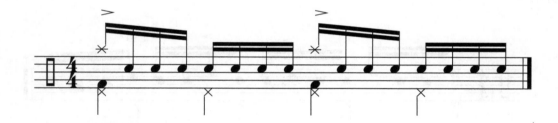

3. **6-2-6-2**

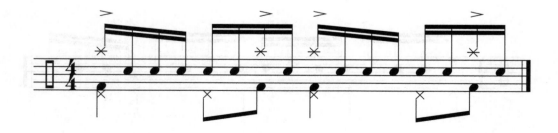

## 4. 3-3-4-6

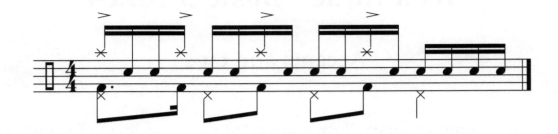

## 5a). 3-3-3-3-4

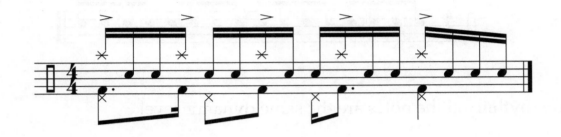

## 5b). 3-3-3-3-2-2

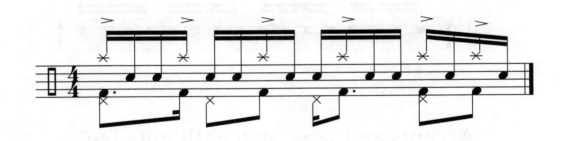

## 5c). 3-3-3-3-3-1

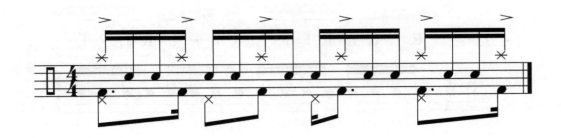

# Part II
# Technique - Basic Strokes

## Accents and taps

When you play a series of notes, if they are all at the same level of sound, you cannot produce a *rhythm*. You can only make rhythm when you start to play some notes louder than others.

For example, here is a bar of sixteenth notes:

There is no rhythm, all the notes are the same dynamic level.

Now here is the same bar with the first note of every four *accented* (loud), and all the other notes *tapped* (quiet):

## Accents and taps, sixteenth note feel

Try all the following exercises, using familiar subdivisions:

1. **4-4-4-4**

grace
(17)

26

## 2. **8-8**

## 3. **6-2-6-2**

## 4. **3-3-4-6**

## 5a). **3-3-3-3-4**

## 5b). **3-3-3-3-2-2**

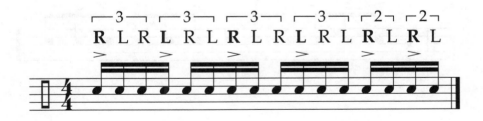

## 5c). **3-3-3-3-3-1**

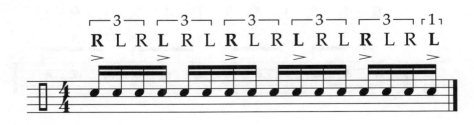

# Accents and taps, triplet feel

1. **3-3-3-3**

2. **6-6**

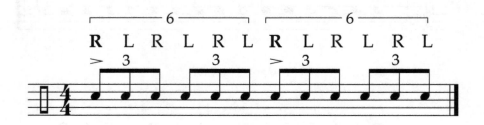

3. **6-2-2-2**

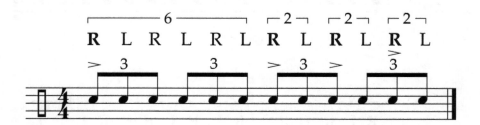

4. **2-2-2-6**

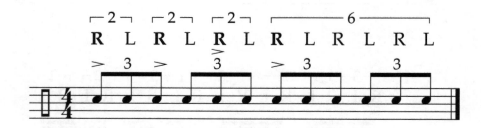

5. **2-2-2-2-2-2**

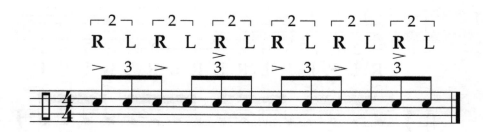

# Accented strokes and upstrokes

It is good technique to proceed an accented stroke with an upward stroke to get the stick into position before the accent is played. Here is a simple exercise to show how this works.

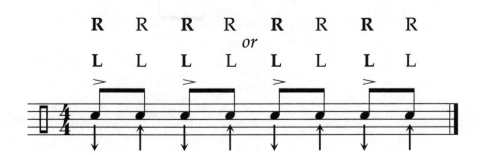

# Basic rock, accents and up strokes

We can start to use this technique immediately by going back to the Basic Rock beats from Drumsense Volume I, and applying accents and upward strokes to the hi hat:

1.

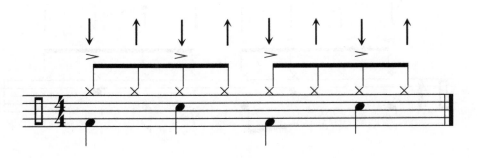

**2.**

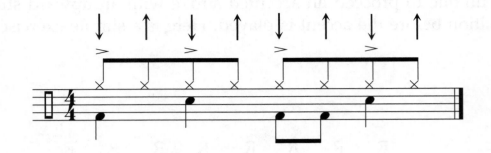

**3.**

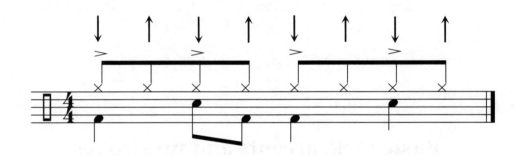

**4.**

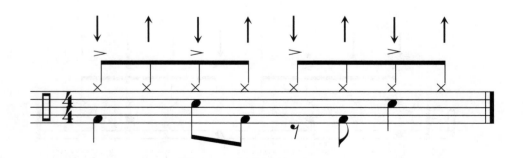

30

# Basic Rock, sixteenth notes on the hi hat, accents and up strokes

1.

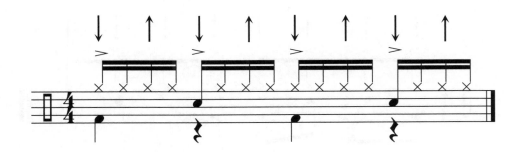

2.

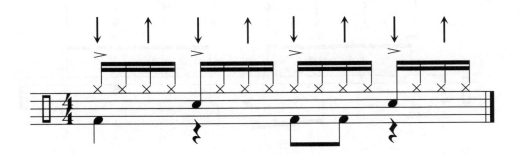

3.

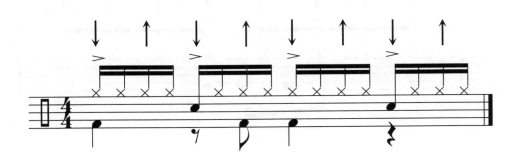

4.

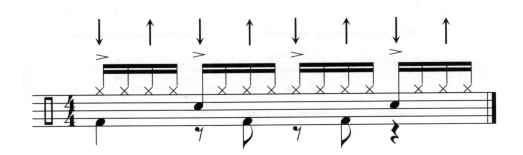

# Bass drum independence, accents and up strokes

1.

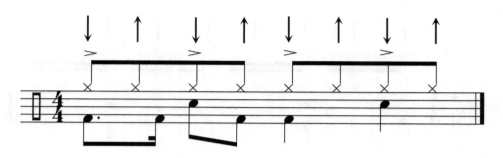

2.

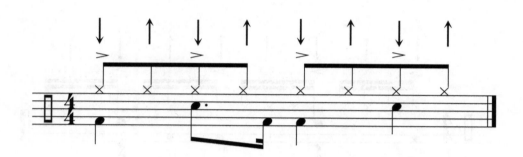

3.

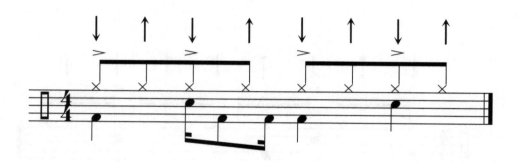

4.

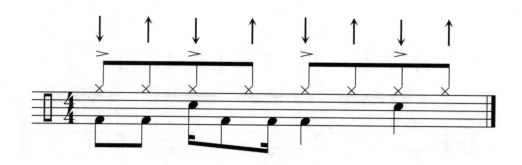

# Bass drum independence, sixteenth notes on the hi hat, accents and up strokes

1.

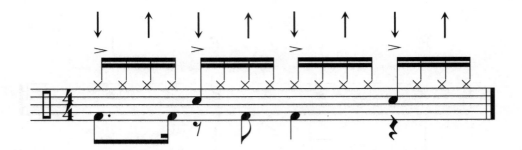

2.

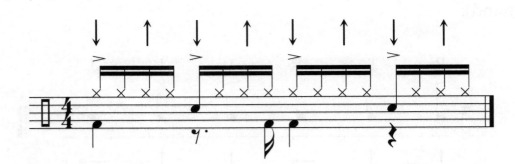

3.

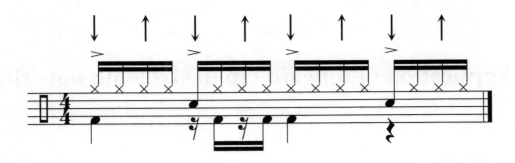

4.

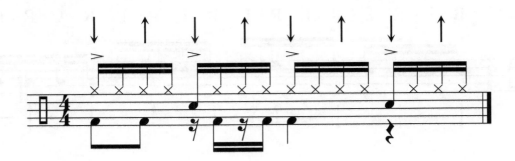

# The use of upward strokes in everyday playing

At the begining of this chapter, we learnt how to use accents and taps in the two basic feels, namely sixteenth notes (two pulse) and triplets (three pulse). Now we should apply the upward stroke, making a group of four notes look like this:

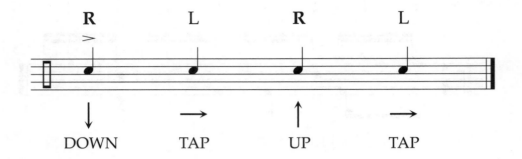

A group of three notes will look like this (we need to play two groups to get back to the leading hand):

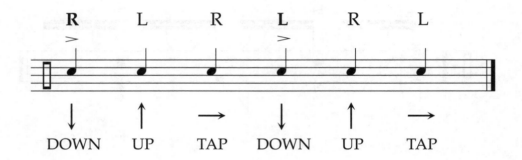

# Application of upward tap in sixteenth note fills

1. **4-4-4-4**
   Around the kit

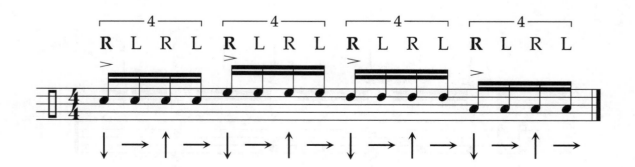

## Accents on toms

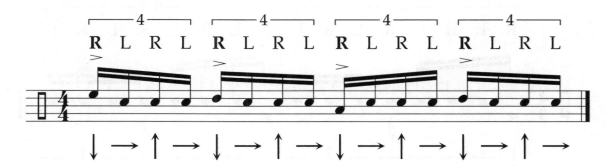

## Accents on cymbals

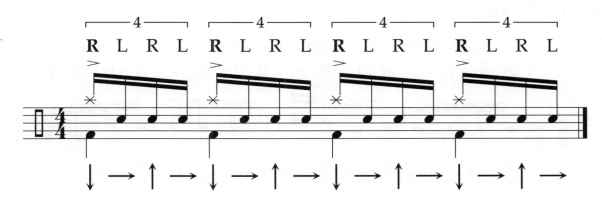

## 2. **8-8**

### Around the kit

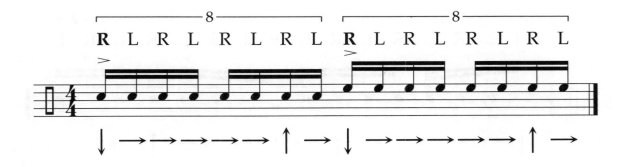

### Accents on toms

Accents on cymbals

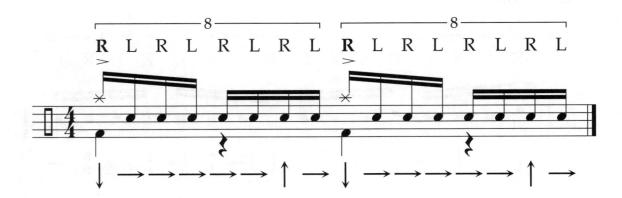

3. **6-2-6-2**

Around the kit

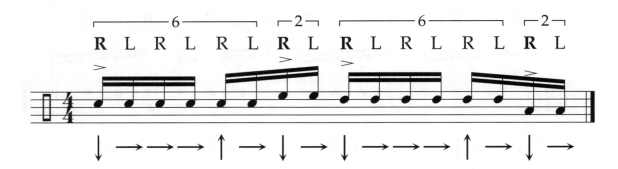

Accents on toms

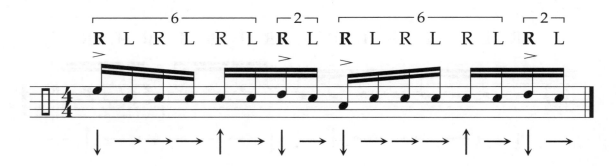

Accents on cymbals

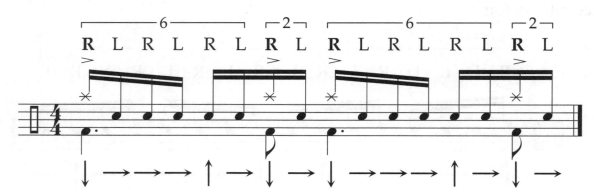

# Application of the Upward Tap in eighth note triplet fills

## 1. 3-3-3-3
### Around the kit

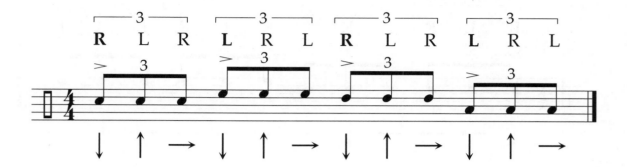

### Accents on toms

### Accents on cymbals

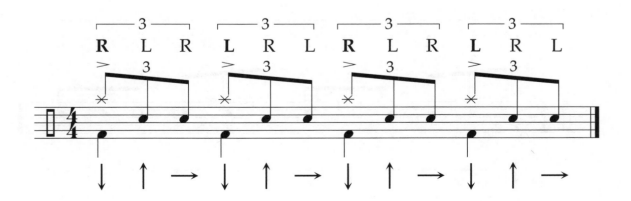

## Around the kit

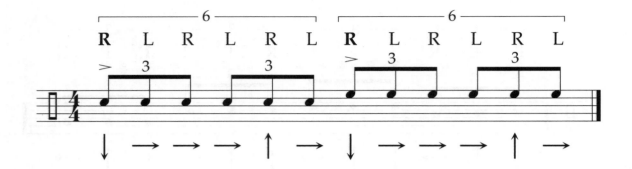

## Accents on toms

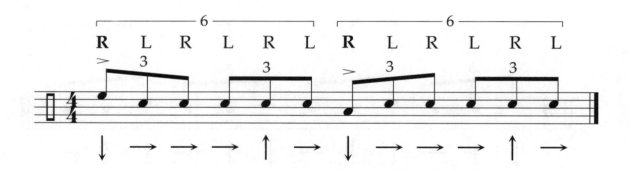

## Accents on cymbals

Work out where the upward taps occur in the following fills:

1. **3-3-3-3-4**

2. **3-3-3-3-3-1**

3. **6-4-2**

4. **4-4-4**

CAMBRIDGE INTRODUCTION TO THE HISTORY OF MANKIND · TOPIC BOOK

GENERAL EDITOR · TREVOR CAIRNS

HUGH ANNAND

# The Rebellion in India, 1857

## F. W. Rawding

**CAMBRIDGE UNIVERSITY PRESS**
Cambridge
London · New York · Melbourne

Published by the Syndics of the Cambridge University Press
The Pitt Building, Trumpington Street, Cambridge CB2 1RP
Bentley House, 200 Euston Road, London NW1 2DB
32 East 57th Street, New York, NY10022, USA
296 Beaconsfield Parade, Middle Park, Melbourne 3206, Australia

© Cambridge University Press 1977

First published 1977

Printed in Great Britain at the
University Press, Cambridge

*Library of Congress cataloguing in publication data*
Rawding, F. W.
The Rebellion in India, 1857.
(Cambridge introduction to the history of mankind: Topic book)
SUMMARY: An account of the establishment of the
English East India Company, the growth of British power
in India, and the 'Mutiny' of 1857 in which the Indian
soldiers in the Bengal Army revolted against their
British officers.
1. India – History – Sepoy Rebellion, 1857–8 – Juv. lit.
[1. India – History – Sepoy Rebellion, 1857–8]
I. Title.
DS478.R23   954.03'17   76-41161
ISBN 0 521 20683 9

## Maps by Reg Piggott

Cover picture: *Men of the 60th Rifles in action outside Delhi
during the siege. They appear to be attacking an encampment
of mutineers near some buildings in the neighbourhood of the
city. It was during the fierce fighting on the Ridge outside Delhi
that a friendship was forged between the 60th Rifles and the
2nd Gurkhas that has lasted to the present day. Colour
lithograph, published 1906, after a contemporary drawing by
Orlando Norie.*

The author and publisher would like to thank the following for
permission to reproduce illustrations:
Cover, pp. 21, 38 National Army Museum; pp. 4, 18 (below)
British Museum; pp. 6, 7, 8, 10, 13, 14, 17, 18 (top), 19, 25, 26, 27,
30, 32, 33, 34 (left), 35 (top right), 37, 39 (top), 45 (below) India
Office Library and Records; pp. 12, 25 (left), 26 (below left), 31
(top), 34 (right), 35 (left), 40, 41, 42, 43, 45 (top right) Cambridge
University Library; p. 15 (left) National Portrait Gallery, London;
p. 15 (right) Victoria and Albert Museum; p. 20 *Military Modelling*
magazine; pp. 23, 26 (below right), 30 (left), 35 (below), 39, 48 (left)
F. W. Rawding; p. 31 Mansell Collection; p. 36 Cassell & Co.,
Ltd; p. 44 Radio Times Hulton Picture Library; p. 46 Haileybury
College; p. 46 (right) Camera and Pen International.
   The drawings on p. 21 by Leslie Marshall.